APPETIZING
HORS D'OEUVRES

D0097175

COLE GROUP

Both U.S. and metric units are provided for all recipes in this book. Ingredients are listed with U.S. units on the left and metric units on the right. The metric quantities have been rounded for ease of use; as a result, in some recipes there may be a slight difference (approximately ½ ounce or 15 grams) between the portion sizes for the two types of measurements.

© 1995 Cole Group, Inc.

Front cover photograph: Joel Glenn

Cole Group, the Cole colophon, and Cole's Cooking Companion are trademarks of Cole Publishing Group, Inc.

Cole Group, Inc.
1330 N. Dutton Ave., Suite 103
Santa Rosa, CA 95401
(800) 959-2717   (707) 526-2682
Fax (707) 526-2687

Printed in Hong Kong

G	F	E	D	C	B	A
1	0	9	8	7	6	5

ISBN 1-56426-808-X

Library of Congress Catalog Card Number 95-23972

Distributed to the book trade by Publishers Group West

Cole books are available for quantity purchases for sales promotions, premiums, fund-raising, or educational use. For more information on *Appetizing Hors d'Oeuvres* or other Cole's Cooking Companion books, please write or call the publisher.

CONTENTS

FESTIVE OVERTURES

*T*he tempting little creature comforts
known as hors d'oeuvres and appetizers
fulfill twin culinary roles: As hors d'oeuvres
(literally "outside the work") they are delightful precursors to a meal; as party fare, they
are the meal. From spur-of-the-moment
nibbles to munch while supper cooks to
an upscale party buffet, the recipes in
Appetizing Hors d'Oeuvres can turn
any occasion into a celebration.

CHOOSING FOOD FOR ENTERTAINING

Carefully prepared and thoughtfully presented, appetizers and hors d'oeuvres are delightful anytime, regardless of the occasion. As a pleasant overture to lunch or dinner, or as the featured attraction at social gatherings, these foods are designed to excite and please the senses, conveying good cheer and hospitality.

Matching the appetizers and hors d'oeuvres you serve with the mood of the occasion is basic to successful entertaining. The foods you enjoy at a barbecue generally won't do for a fancy reception. For formal events, serve elegant-looking foods that won't fall apart, drip onto guests' clothing, or otherwise be difficult to handle. Save anything messy or unwieldy for casual gatherings.

Choose food that complements the setting. If there's not room enough to provide all the guests a place to sit, the best option is dips, spreads, and other finger foods that can be picked up and eaten with no fuss. The food can be passed around on trays or offered at strategic points around the room, with napkins and perhaps small plates alongside. If there's room enough to seat everyone, you can include plated hors d'oeuvres and appetizers that require silverware. Here's an overview of the three categories of foods presented in this book:

Dips and Dippers A little something smooth, creamy, and delicious on a cracker or crudité is one of the most popular kinds of appetizers and hors d'oeuvres. Foods that otherwise might be messy to eat without a knife and fork can be blended, seasoned, and served as a dip or spread in a dish, crock, or handsome mold. Of course, good bread, crackers, fresh vegetables, and other accompaniments are an essential part of the equation. Best of all, most of the foods in this category can be prepared in advance.

For small, informal gatherings, set out a pâté or creamy dip alongside little toasts in a basket or an artful composition of fresh vegetables and let guests help themselves. For larger

stand-up gatherings, serve ready-to-eat canapés that can be arranged on trays to be circulated among your guests.

Pick-Ups Savory morsels that are easily managed with the fingers, pick-ups are favorites with anyone who's ever tried balancing a slippery fork on a tiny plate in a crowded room. Depending on what you're serving, consider setting out small baskets or bowls for easy disposal of debris—wooden skewers, cocktail picks, or bones from chicken wings or ribs.

Offer plenty of napkins but don't be surprised if you see some licking of fingertips any time pick-ups are within reach of hungry guests. If you're not using plates, be sure any hot foods you serve aren't so piping hot they could burn fingers or lips. Foods intended for serving cold should be nicely chilled. Good food you can pick up and enjoy on the spot disappears fast, so plan to have extras in reserve.

Plate Food Elaborate canapés and open-face sandwiches, succulent seafood dishes, deliciously messy pizzas—all the wonderful foods that can be awkward to eat out of hand in a social setting are nicely managed with plates and forks. Many of these foods make ideal appetizers or first courses for a sit-down meal.

The size and type of tableware you use depends on what you're serving, as well as the setting and the mood you want to create.

If the guests can all be seated, use whatever suits the occasion and pleases you. Disposable utensils are usually fine for casual outdoor dining and other informal occasions, especially if young children are present. If there's standing room only for your guests, keep in mind the tendency of paper plates to go limp under sauces, salads, and other moist foods, or with anything that requires considerable cutting. If you choose throwaway dinnerware, have a good supply available so you can offer fresh replacements as they're needed. China and silverware are easiest for guests to use; set up trays to hold dirty dishes and utensils until they can be carried into the kitchen.

SERVE IT WITH FLAIR

As any professional chef or caterer knows, the difference between good food and great food is a matter of presentation. The best cooks know how to "style" food, to present it in such a way that it's irresistible. They know how to use props like baskets and flowers to best effect, and they are constantly on the lookout for imaginative serving ideas. Many of the tricks of the catering trade are perfectly suited to home entertaining.

When you're rummaging through the cabinets looking for serving dishes for entertaining, be creative! Instead of a dish, how about an unusual vase or pitcher that you could use for nuts, chips, or olives? Or a teapot or mug you could fill with skewered foods? Tiny Japanese sake cups or goblets make ideal containers for seafood. Try using small terra cotta flowerpots to hold crudités. You can even use a good-looking cardboard gift box lined with tissue or bright napkins to hold muffins, breads, crackers, or little sandwiches.

Baskets and trays of various shapes and sizes make handsome containers for buffets or for passing at the table. You can fill baskets with napkin-wrapped or ribbon-tied silverware or with edible "still lifes" of fresh vegetables or fruits.

Whatever you serve your guests—from a simple plate of cheese and crackers to party food fit for royals—serve it with flair.

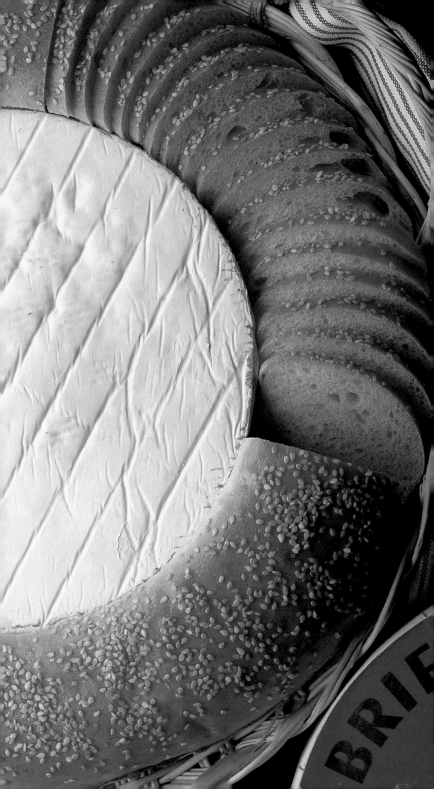

RECIPES AND TECHNIQUES

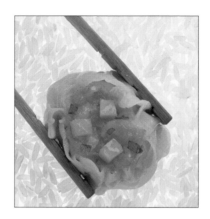

Whether you're preparing hors d'oeuvres
for a few friends or a few hundred, the foods
you select set the tone and mood for the
occasion. Generate an elegant ambiance with
a platter of fresh fruit and luscious Rum-
Chocolate Dipping Sauce (see page 36), or
make the atmosphere relaxed but festive by
offering a classic Mediterranean mezze
(see photo on opposite page). Whatever the
event, use the recipes and techniques in
Appetizing Hors d'Oeuvres to create a
convivial atmosphere.

DIPS AND DIPPERS

Few gestures convey hospitality as readily as offering a generous array of dips, spreads, and suitable accompaniments. Dunking crisp vegetables into a creamy blend of cheese and egg (see page 14), swirling rice cakes through a spicy Asian dip (see page 24), spreading baked Brie (see page 34) onto homemade crumpets (see page 28)—simple pleasures like these are the focus of this section.

CREAM CHEESE-EGG DIP

Serve this fluffy dip with an assortment of crudités, crisp crackers, or bread. Using a microwave is the quickest way to prepare the hard-cooked eggs for this recipe, but you can also prepare them in the traditional way: Place the uncooked eggs in a small saucepan and cover them with cold water. Bring water to a boil, cover, and immediately remove the pan from the heat. Let stand 30 minutes, then crack, peel, and use as directed in the recipe.

as needed	oil	as needed
2	eggs	2
1 package (8 oz)	cream cheese	1 package (225 g)
2 tbl	milk	2 tbl
2 tbl	bottled mayonnaise	2 tbl
1 tsp	prepared mustard	1 tsp
½ tsp	cumin	½ tsp
¼ tsp	salt	¼ tsp
as needed	parsley, for garnish	as needed

1. Lightly oil a small microwave-safe dish. Break 1 egg into dish and puncture yolk with tines of a fork. Cover dish and microwave on full power until yolk is firm (1–1½ minutes). Place egg in food processor or in blender; repeat procedure with second egg.

2. To cooked eggs add cream cheese, milk, mayonnaise, mustard, cumin, and salt. Process until fluffy.

3. Transfer mixture to a small bowl. Garnish with parsley.

Makes 1½ cups (350 ml).

BOUCHERON DIP

Goat cheese adds its distinctive tang to this creamy dip. Serve with artichoke hearts, mushrooms, and red and green bell peppers.

1 cup	plain yogurt	250 ml
2 oz	Boucheron cheese or other mild fresh goat cheese	60 g
¼ cup	sour cream	60 ml
1 tbl	minced fresh chives, dill, thyme or chervil, for garnish	1 tbl

1. Line a sieve with cheesecloth and set it over a bowl. Spoon yogurt into sieve and let drain 2 hours.

2. Force the cheese through a coarse strainer. Stir in drained yogurt and the sour cream. Garnish with fresh minced herbs before serving.

Makes approximately 1¼ cups (300 ml).

THAI SWEET GARLIC DIPPING SAUCE

Serve this dipping sauce with crudités or Lacy Egg Net Pillows (see page 39) and other fried appetizers. Based on the classic Chinese sweet-and-sour sauce (but considerably hotter), it can be prepared in advance and kept for several weeks in a covered jar in the refrigerator. The Thai fish sauce is available in most Asian markets.

½ cup	sugar	125 ml
¾ cup	red wine vinegar	175 ml
1 tbl	Thai fish sauce	1 tbl
1 tsp	tomato paste (optional)	1 tsp
2	dried red chiles coarsely chopped	2
4 cloves	garlic, bruised	4 cloves
1	carrot, julienned, for garnish	1
¼ cup	chopped peanuts	60 ml

1. In a small stainless steel saucepan, combine ½ cup water, sugar, vinegar, fish sauce, tomato paste (if used), chiles, and garlic.

2. Bring to a boil, reduce heat, and boil slowly until sauce is consistency of thin syrup (about 10 minutes).

3. Strain and cool. Blend in carrot and peanuts.

Makes 1 cup (250 ml).

PREPARING CRUDITÉS

Choice vegetables for crudités platters include cherry tomatoes, celery and carrot sticks, jicama slices, red or green bell pepper strips, small chiles, green onions, snow peas, diagonal slices of summer squash or zucchini, whole button mushrooms, and Belgian endive spears. Briefly blanching vegetables such as broccoli and cauliflower florets or asparagus tips tenderizes and sweetens them.

SALSA CRUDA SABROSA

This salsa is best when freshly made.

1	yellow onion, peeled and minced	1
3	ripe tomatoes, peeled, seeded, and coarsely chopped	3
2 tbl	minced cilantro (coriander leaves)	2 tbl
1 clove	garlic, minced	1 clove
1	green chile, minced, or more to taste	1
1 tbl	fresh lime juice	1 tbl
to taste	salt	to taste

In a small bowl combine all ingredients except salt no more than 1 hour before serving. Add salt just before serving.

Makes ¾ cup (175 ml).

FIESTA GUACAMOLE

Serve this festive dip with crudités.

2	avocados	2
2 tsp	fresh lime or lemon juice	2 tsp
¼ cup	sour cream (optional)	60 ml
1 clove	garlic, crushed	1 clove
1	tomato, diced	1
1	canned jalapeño pepper, seeded and finely chopped	1
¼ cup	onion, finely minced	60 ml
to taste	cilantro (coriander leaves), coarsely chopped	to taste

Halve the avocados; remove pits, scoop out pulp, and mash with a fork. Add lime juice, sour cream (if used), garlic, tomato, jalapeño, onion, and cilantro, mixing after each addition. Serve at room temperature or lightly chilled.

Makes 2½ cups (600 ml).

GREEK OLIVE TAPENADE

Spread this tangy relish on toasted bread rounds for a colorful, eye-catching hors d'oeuvre. It can be made a week in advance; store in a covered jar in the refrigerator, with a thin film of olive oil on top of the tapenade to help preserve color and flavor.

1 lb	imported black olives, preferably Greek Kalamata, pitted and finely chopped	450 g
1 cup	green pimiento-stuffed olives, finely chopped	250 ml
½ cup	diced red bell pepper	125 ml
¼ cup	minced parsley	60 ml
2 tbl	minced garlic	2 tbl
3 tbl	finely minced anchovy fillets	3 tbl
2 tbl	minced fresh oregano	2 tbl
½ cup	olive oil	125 ml
to taste	freshly ground black pepper	to taste
as needed	toasted bread rounds or pita-bread triangles	as needed

1. In a large bowl combine black and green olives, red pepper, parsley, garlic, anchovies, oregano, olive oil, and black pepper.

2. Cover and marinate overnight in the refrigerator. Serve with toasted bread rounds or toasted pita-bread triangles.

Makes 3 cups (700 ml).

Artichokes for Two

A pair of artichokes at their prime makes an excellent appetizer for a candlelit dinner for two, but you can easily double or triple the recipe for a larger gathering.

Curry Mayonnaise

1 tbl	olive oil	1 tbl
¼ tsp	curry powder	¼ tsp
¼ cup	mayonnaise	60 ml
1 tsp	lemon juice	1 tsp

Herbed Vinaigrette

pinch	salt and freshly ground black pepper	pinch
1 tbl	tarragon-flavored wine vinegar	1 tbl
4 tbl	olive oil	4 tbl
1 tbl	minced fresh tarragon, basil, dill, or chervil (or a mixture of several herbs)	1 tbl
2	steamed artichokes (see page 21)	2

1. To prepare mayonnaise, in a small skillet heat oil over low heat. Add curry powder and cook 2–3 minutes. Allow to cool, then stir into mayonnaise. Add lemon juice to taste and set aside in refrigerator. Flavor will improve if allowed to stand several hours.

2. To prepare vinaigrette, add salt and pepper to vinegar. Whisk in oil and blend in minced herbs. Taste and adjust seasoning if needed. Set aside.

3. Place artichokes on serving tray, accompanied by mayonnaise and vinaigrette. Serve warm or chilled.

Serves 2.

Preparing Artichokes for Appetizers

From young buds the size of walnuts to mature buds bigger than a baseball, steamed artichokes make terrific appetizers.

To prepare artichokes for steaming, trim off any thorny tips of outer leaves with scissors or a paring knife. Snap or cut off smallest leaves close to stem. Rub freshly cut parts with lemon to prevent discoloration. Slice stem off to form flat bottom. Set artichoke stem side down on a steamer above at least 1 inch (2.5 cm) of boiling water. Cover and steam until bases are tender (30–60 minutes, depending on size).

Serve the artichokes whole (see page 20) or use either of the following techniques.

To prepare artichoke cups, use large artichokes. After steaming carefully spread outer leaves to expose heart. Remove small heart leaves and scrape out fuzzy choke with a spoon. Fill hollow with a sauce for dipping outer leaves or a shrimp salad with herbed mayonnaise.

To prepare artichoke bottoms, use large artichokes. After steaming remove all leaves and scrape away choke, leaving a shallow cup that can be used to hold ingredients such as poached eggs, oysters, or chicken salad.

Mushroom-Liver Pâté

Prepare the pâté a day before you intend to use it and serve cold. Serve it directly from the mold or unmold and serve on a platter.

1 tbl	olive oil	1 tbl
1 tbl	butter	1 tbl
1	onion, chopped	1
2 cloves	garlic, minced	2 cloves
½ lb	chicken livers, rinsed and dried	225 g
½ lb	fresh mushrooms, sliced	225 g
3 tbl	minced parsley	3 tbl
1 tsp	salt	1 tsp
¼ tsp	freshly ground black pepper	¼ tsp
1 tbl	brandy	1 tbl
as needed	parsley or trumpet chanterelles, for garnish	as needed
as needed	crackers, for accompaniment	as needed

1. In a saucepan over medium-high heat combine oil and butter. Add onion and garlic and sauté 3–4 minutes, stirring frequently.

2. Add chicken livers and mushrooms. Cook until livers lose their pink color (3–4 minutes), stirring occasionally. Drain off and discard liquid.

3. Transfer mixture to food processor or blender. Add minced parsley, salt, pepper, and brandy. Process until smooth. Pour into a 2-cup (500 ml) mold, cover, and chill at least 4 hours, or overnight.

4. Garnish with parsley and serve with crackers.

Makes 2 cups (500 ml).

TAMARIND SHRIMP DIP WITH RICE CAKES

In this fascinating Thai version of chips and dip, spicy flavors are mellowed with the richness of coconut cream. Tamarind water, rice cakes, and Thai fish sauce are available in most Asian markets.

1 can (14 oz)	unsweetened coconut milk	1 can (425 ml)
1 tsp	black peppercorns	1 tsp
3 cloves	garlic, peeled	3 cloves
1 bunch	cilantro (fresh coriander), roots intact	1 bunch
4	shallots, sliced	4
½ cup	chopped roasted peanuts	125 ml
½ lb	ground or minced chicken	225 g
6 oz	shrimp, shelled, deveined, and coarsely chopped	170 g
2	fresh red chiles	2
2 tbl	firmly packed brown sugar	2 tbl
2 tbl	Thai fish sauce	2 tbl
3 tbl	tamarind water	3 tbl
12	rice cakes	12

1. Without shaking can, pour coconut milk into a tall glass container and set aside until coconut cream rises to top (1–2 hours). Skim off ½ cup (125 ml) cream, place in a small bowl, and set aside. Reserve milk in glass.

2. Grind peppercorns; chop 1 of the garlic cloves with 1 tablespoon coriander root. Mix and set aside.

3. Place reserved coconut cream in wok over medium-high heat and cook until thick and oily (about 2 minutes), stirring continuously. Add reserved peppercorn mixture and fry until fragrant (about 30 seconds).

4. Slice the remaining 2 garlic cloves and add to wok along with shallots and peanuts; stir-fry until shallots are lightly browned (about 1 minute). Add chicken, shrimp, and one of the chiles, chopped; stir-fry until shrimp turns pink (2–3 minutes). Add brown sugar, fish sauce, and tamarind water; cook together 1 minute. Add reserved coconut milk and cook, stirring constantly, until liquid is reduced to the consistency of light cream and is caramel colored. Transfer to a saucer. Garnish with cilantro leaves (discard stems) and remaining chile, slivered. Arrange rice cakes around dip.

Serves 6.

Lomi-Lomi Salmon

This marinated fish appetizer features salmon, which early missionaries introduced to the Hawaiian islanders.

1 lb	salmon fillet, skinned and cubed	450 g
1	cucumber, peeled, seeded, and diced	1
2	tomatoes, peeled, seeded, and diced	2
½ cup	minced red onion	125 ml
2	green onions, minced	2
½ cup	fresh lime juice	125 ml
2 tbl	olive oil	2 tbl
to taste	salt and freshly ground black pepper	to taste
⅓ cup	minced cilantro (coriander leaves)	85 ml
as needed	toasted bread rounds	as needed
as needed	sliced onion rings, for garnish	as needed

1. In a stainless steel, ceramic, or glass bowl, combine salmon, cucumber, tomatoes, red and green onions, lime juice, and olive oil. Stir gently, cover, and let marinate, refrigerated, for 1–24 hours.

2. Remove salmon from refrigerator 30 minutes before serving. Season to taste with salt and pepper; stir in cilantro. Serve on toasted bread rounds. Garnish with onion rings.

Serves 12.

Planning for Variety

Aside from great taste, an array of appetizers should reflect an interesting variety of shapes, colors, and textures. Plan to offer a few hot hors d'oeuvres, a few cold, a few at room temperature. Create visual appeal by including both round and long, thin shapes on the same platter. An assortment of foods with warm colors—red, orange, yellow—and cool—green or purple—make an alluring combination. Finally, be sure to serve foods with different textures: crisp, soft, crunchy, velvety, chewy, smooth.

BLUE CHEESE-ALMOND CRISPS

With a food processor you can prepare the dough for these appetizers in less than 5 minutes. The crackers are best eaten just out of the oven. Lining the baking sheet with parchment paper keeps the crackers from burning.

1 cup	unbleached flour	250 ml
½ tsp	salt	½ tsp
2 cloves	garlic	2 cloves
⅛ tsp	cayenne pepper	⅛ tsp
2 tbl	Parmesan cheese	2 tbl
4 oz	blue cheese	115 g
6 tbl	cold butter	6 tbl
6 tbl	water	6 tbl
1	egg	1
¼ cup	finely chopped almonds	60 ml

1. Place flour, salt, garlic, cayenne, and Parmesan cheese in a food processor. Turn on and off to combine. Add blue cheese and butter. Turn on and off to combine. Add 3–4 tablespoons of the water gradually, with machine running. Stop machine when dough holds together.

2. Roll dough into a cylinder about 1½ inches (3.75 cm) in diameter, and wrap it in aluminum foil. Chill for 2 hours, or freeze if serving at another time.

3. Preheat oven to 400°F (205°C) when ready to bake. Beat egg with 2 tablespoons of the water to form an egg wash. Brush half the egg wash onto the exterior of the cylinder of dough. Roll in almonds. Slice into rounds of dough about ¼ inch (.6 cm) thick. Place on a parchment-lined baking sheet. Brush circles with remaining egg wash.

4. Bake for 12–14 minutes. Cool on a baking rack.

Makes 16 crackers.

COCKTAIL CRUMPETS

Serve this traditional English favorite toasted, buttered, and accompanied by smoked meats or sliced Cheddar and an assortment of mustards and chutneys.

1 package	active dry yeast	1 package
1 tsp	sugar	1 tsp
¾ cup	warm water (about 105°F or 41°C)	175 ml
¾ tsp	salt	¾ tsp
2 tbl	unsalted butter, melted	2 tbl
½ cup	milk, scalded and cooled to room temperature	125 ml
1¼ cups	unbleached flour	300 ml
½ tsp	baking soda	½ tsp
1 tbl	boiling water	1 tbl

1. Dissolve yeast and sugar in the warm water. Let proof 10 minutes. Then add salt, butter, and milk and mix well. Add flour all at once and beat steadily for at least 4 minutes. Cover with a warm damp towel and let rise in a warm place until doubled.

2. Combine baking soda with the boiling water. Add to batter and stir until completely blended. Cover and let rise again until doubled.

3. Lightly butter crumpet rings or clean, empty tuna cans (7-ounce or 200-g size, with both ends removed). Heat a nonstick skillet. Place 3 or 4 rings in skillet. Put a rounded tablespoon of batter in each.

4. Cover skillet and cook until a light crust forms on top of crumpets, about 5 minutes. Remove cover and turn crumpets. Cook a few minutes more, uncovered, to brown second side. Set aside to cool and cook remaining batter. Toast before serving.

Makes 24 crumpets.

CORN DOLLARS

These rich cornmeal pancakes (see photo on cover) taste delicious topped with sour cream and Salsa Cruda Sabrosa (see page 16).

1½ cups	unbleached flour	350 ml
½ cup	cornmeal	½ cup
1 tsp	baking powder	1 tsp
6	eggs, separated	6
6 oz	cream cheese	170 g
1½ cups	milk	350 ml
½ cup	unsalted butter, melted	125 ml
¼ cup	minced green onion	60 ml
1 cup	fresh corn kernels cut from cob	250 ml
2 tsp	salt	2 tsp
to taste	hot-pepper sauce	to taste
as needed	butter and peanut oil, for frying	as needed
as needed	Salsa Cruda Sabrosa (see page 16)	as needed
as needed	sour cream	as needed

1. Sift together flour, cornmeal, and baking powder. In large bowl of electric mixer, cream egg yolks and cream cheese. Add cornmeal mixture, then slowly add milk. Stir in melted butter, green onions, corn kernels, salt, and hot-pepper sauce to taste.

2. In a separate bowl beat egg whites with a pinch of salt until they are stiff but not dry. Fold a third of the whites into batter. Then gently fold batter into remaining whites.

3. Lightly oil a nonstick frying pan with 1 teaspoon each butter and peanut oil. Heat pan until butter foams. Drop batter into hot fat by rounded tablespoons and cook until bubbles form and burst on top. Turn cakes over and cook an additional 30 seconds. Transfer cakes to a warm platter and dot with salsa, sour cream, or both.

Makes 60 dollar-sized pancakes.

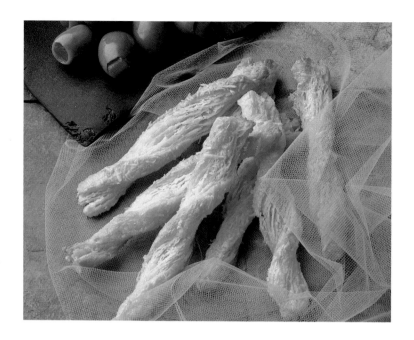

PARMESAN TWISTS

Delicious served with dips, spreads, salads, and soups, or on their own as a cocktail nibble, these twists can be baked ahead, cooled, and frozen. Refresh in a 350°F (175°C) oven for 5–8 minutes.

1 recipe	Quick Puff Pastry (see page 79)	1 recipe
1	egg, beaten	1
½ cup	freshly grated Parmesan cheese	125 ml

1. Roll Quick Puff Pastry ⅜ inch (1 cm) thick; brush with egg and sprinkle with ¼ cup (60 ml) Parmesan cheese. Lightly press pastry with a rolling pin. Turn over. Cover with remaining Parmesan cheese; press with rolling pin.

2. Cut pastry sheets into 24 strips, each ¾ inch (1.9 cm) wide. Twist gently and place on parchment-lined baking sheets. Chill 30 minutes. Preheat oven to 425°F (220°C). Bake until golden brown and crisp (about 12 minutes).

Makes 24 twists.

STILTON CROCK WITH PORT WINE

A wedge of blue-veined Stilton cheese and a decanter of port are a venerable British tradition. This pair can be blended and packed into a handsome crock for a predinner spread, the flavors melding during the course of a week-long aging. For a large holiday gathering, order a whole wheel of Stilton (10 lb or 4.6 kg) and serve it as the centerpiece of an hors d'oeuvres buffet. Slice off the top and scoop out the cheese, leaving a sturdy wall all around. Then blend the cheese with a bottle of port, pack the wheel with the cheese mixture, and replace the cover for aging.

2 lb	Stilton cheese	900 g
⅓–½ cup	imported port	85–125 ml
as needed	crackers, for accompaniment	as needed

1. Trim any rind from cheese; place cheese in a bowl. Add port. With back of a wooden spoon, blend port and cheese. Pack into a 4-cup (900 ml) crock, cover with plastic wrap, refrigerate, and let age 1 week.

2. Bring cheese to room temperature and serve with crackers.

Makes 4 cups (900 ml), about 20 cocktail servings.

SWEET BRIE BRULÉE

Brie lovers and anyone with a sweet tooth will particularly appreciate this novel appetizer. Use a quiche dish and circle it with baguette slices or crackers for easy serving. Ripe brie, which is smooth and creamy throughout, is essential for the success of this recipe. The texture of the brie should be soft but not excessively runny; if it is chalky in the middle, the brie is underripe.

1 wheel (8 oz)	Brie	1 wheel (225 g)
½ cup	chopped pecans or walnuts	125 ml
¾ cup	firmly packed brown sugar	175 ml
as needed	sliced baguette or crackers, for accompaniment	as needed

1. Preheat oven to 400°F (205°C). Unwrap Brie and place in an ovenproof quiche dish or pie plate. Sprinkle with nuts. Cover top and sides with brown sugar, gently patting surface with fingers to coat. Do not be concerned if sides are not fully covered.

2. Bake just until cheese is warm and soft (about 5–7 minutes), testing with a toothpick. Cheese should retain shape. Serve immediately with baguette slices or crackers.

Makes 1 cup (250 ml).

Rum-Chocolate Dipping Sauce

*Serve the chocolate sauce in a heated ceramic pot to keep it warm.
Around it arrange items for dipping: squares of pound cake (or angel
food), ladyfingers, madeleines, thin sugar cookies, and fresh fruit. In
addition to apples, pears, and strawberries, try halved apricots,
banana chunks, quartered figs, melon wedges, sliced peaches and
nectarines, orange sections, and seedless grapes.*

½ cup	whipping cream	125 ml
8 oz	semisweet chocolate, finely chopped	225 g
1 tsp	vanilla extract	1 tsp
2 tbl	rum	2 tbl
1	pound cake	1
2	apples	2
2	pears	2
1	lemon, juiced	1
1 pint	strawberries	500 ml

1. Place cream in 1-quart (900-l) saucepan; slowly heat. As
   soon as cream begins to form bubbles around edge, turn off
   heat and whisk in chocolate. When chocolate is completely
   melted, stir in vanilla and rum. Set aside.

2. Cut pound cake, apples, and pears into 1½-inch (3.75-cm)
   cubes. Drizzle lemon juice over apples and pears. Wash and
   dry strawberries. Arrange cake and fruit on a platter.

3. Place chocolate mixture into a ceramic or metal fondue pot
   and set over a lighted candle or other low heat source. Heat
   until chocolate is warm but not bubbling. Provide fondue
   forks or bamboo skewers for dipping cake and fruit into
   chocolate sauce.

Serves 6.

PICK-UPS

Easy to handle without plates or forks and gone in a flash, pick-ups are ideal party fare. Besides unusual offerings like Italian-style cheese fritters (see page 56) and Cajun shrimp in corn-meal batter (see page 60), this section includes tips for almost effortless appetizers and hors d'oeuvres (see pages 55 and 61).

LACY EGG NET PILLOWS

Originating in Thailand, these delicate wrappers encase a tasty pork filling to create attractive little pillows bursting with flavor. The Thai fish sauce for these appetizers is available in most Asian markets.

2 cloves	garlic	2 cloves
1 tsp	whole black peppercorns	1 tsp
1 bunch	cilantro (fresh coriander), roots intact	1 bunch
2 tbl	peanut oil	2 tbl
2	shallots, minced	2
¾ lb	pork butt, minced	350 g
1½ tbl	Thai fish sauce	1½ tbl
2 tsp	firmly packed brown sugar	2 tsp
2 tbl	chopped roasted peanuts	2 tbl
6	eggs	6
3	red serrano chiles, seeded and slivered	3
1 recipe	Thai Sweet Garlic Dipping Sauce (see page 15), for accompaniment	1 recipe

1. Chop garlic, crush peppercorns, and mince enough coriander root to make 1 tablespoon. Combine and set aside. Discard cilantro stems and reserve leaves for garnish.

2. Preheat wok over medium-high heat until hot. Pour in 1 tablespoon of the oil; then add garlic mixture and shallots and stir-fry until oil is fragrant (about 30 seconds). Add pork and stir-fry until browned (about 2 minutes). Add fish sauce and brown sugar; cook until liquid is completely reduced. Mix in peanuts. Remove to a bowl and set aside.

3. Beat eggs with 3 tablespoons water and pour mixture into a shallow plate; set aside. Preheat a 7- to 8-inch (17.5- to 20-cm) nonstick skillet over medium heat until hot. Pour in the remaining 1 tablespoon oil. With several rolled-up paper towels, spread oil in skillet and wipe up excess; set towels aside. Prepare egg nets (see page 41), removing each net to a work surface as it is cooked, wiping skillet with oiled towels, and repeating with remaining egg mixture to make 8 nets.

4. Cut each egg net in half. In center of each egg net half place 1 cilantro leaf and a chile sliver. Top with 1 tablespoon pork mixture. Fold over bottom, turn in sides, and roll into a small pillow. Place, seam down, on a serving plate. Repeat with remaining egg nets. Garnish with more chile slivers and cilantro leaves; serve with dipping sauce.

Makes 16 pillows.

Making Egg Nets

These decorative little jackets, made of beaten egg, make delicate wrappers for Asian foods. The beaten egg may also be drizzled into hot oil, fried until golden brown and crunchy, and torn into pieces to be used for garnishing.

1. Flatten your hand and dip your fingers and palm into beaten egg mixture (see recipe on page 39).

2. Spread fingers and, holding them 2 inches (5 cm) above skillet, wave your hand back and forth across full width of skillet, letting egg drip from fingertips in fine threads. Repeat until bottom of skillet is covered with egg threads. Then, with same motion, wave fingers back and forth across skillet at right angle to first threads, repeating several times to form a fine netting.

3. Cook until egg is set and light yellow. With the edge of a spatula, carefully lift edges of net and remove from skillet. The entire process for each net takes 2–3 minutes. Cut, fill, and roll nets according to recipe directions.

MELON-PROSCIUTTO WRAPS

Paper-thin prosciutto and fragrant melon combine for a salty-sweet taste experience that is unforgettable. For a change of pace, substitute spears of papaya, pear, or mango for the melon—or serve them all, complemented by a crisp, cold white wine.

1	ripe, sweet melon of any variety	1
½	lemon	½
6 oz	prosciutto, sliced paper-thin	170 g
as needed	freshly ground black pepper	as needed
as needed	olive oil (optional)	as needed
1 tbl	minced parsley, for garnish	1 tbl

1. If using melon, cut away rind, then halve melon lengthwise. Scoop out seeds, then cut each half in half horizontally. Slice each quarter into pieces about ½ inch (1.25 cm) wide. If using papayas, pears, or mangoes, peel fruit, remove cores or seeds, and slice into spears about ½ inch (1.25 cm) wide. Rub pears lightly with lemon to prevent browning.

2. Wrap melon with prosciutto slices, allowing ends of fruit to show. Arrange on a serving platter. Dust with pepper, drizzle lightly with olive oil (if used), and garnish with parsley.

Serves 12.

Endive Spears with Gorgonzola and Walnuts

Stunning in presentation, this delicious appetizer is effortless to prepare.

24 spears	Belgian endive	24 spears
as needed	Gorgonzola cheese	as needed
24	toasted walnut halves	24

1. Wash and pat dry 24 endive spears.

2. Place ½ teaspoon Gorgonzola cheese on each spear and garnish with 1 large toasted walnut half. Serve chilled.

Serves 8.

Steamed Potatoes with Sour Cream and Caviar

In this visually attractive hors d'oeuvre, caviar gives some pizazz to potatoes filled with sour cream.

2 lb	tiny red-skinned potatoes	900 g
as needed	sour cream	as needed
as needed	tiny caviar	as needed

1. Steam potatoes until tender when pierced with a knife (30–35 minutes). Cool slightly.

2. Using a melon ball cutter, scoop a small ball of flesh from the top of each potato. Fill with 1 teaspoon sour cream and dot with tiny caviar. Serve chilled.

Serves 8.

GARLIC-PEPPER ALMONDS

Peppery toasted almonds make a convenient nibble to accompany soft drinks or wine. The mixture can be made ahead and stored in an airtight container.

2 tbl	olive oil	2 tbl
2 tbl	butter	2 tbl
1 tbl	minced garlic	1 tbl
½ tsp	hot-pepper flakes	½ tsp
3 cups	whole blanched almonds	700 ml
as needed	salt	as needed

In a large skillet over moderate heat, combine oil and butter. When butter foams, add garlic and stir until fragrant. Add pepper flakes and stir 15 seconds. Add almonds and stir continuously until nuts are well coated and lightly toasted. Salt to taste. Drain nuts on paper towels and let cool before serving.

Makes 3 cups (700 ml).

OLIVES IN CITRUS-FENNEL MARINADE

Overnight marinating infuses these olives with the flavors of tangy citrus peel, garlic, and fennel.

2 lb	black olives, rinsed of any brine	900 g
4	lemons, juiced	4
2	oranges, rind only, cut into strips	2
2	lemons, rind only, cut into strips	2
3–4 tbl	fennel seeds	3–4 tbl
4 cloves	garlic, peeled	4 cloves

Combine olives, lemon juice, orange and lemon rind, fennel seeds, and garlic. Pack into jars, cover, and marinate overnight at room temperature. Serve chilled.

Makes 2 pounds (900 g).

FOCACCIA WITH ONIONS AND PANCETTA

Caramelized red onions top this Italian flatbread.

2 packages	active dry yeast	2 packages
½ cup	warm water (about 105°F or 41°C)	125 ml
3 cups	unbleached flour	700 ml
1 cup	warm milk	250 ml
¼ cup	olive oil	60 ml
½ lb	pancetta or bacon, thinly sliced	225 g
2	sweet red onions, thinly sliced	2
1 tbl	sugar	1 tbl
¼ cup	freshly grated Parmesan cheese	60 ml
as needed	freshly ground black pepper	as needed

1. To prepare dough, dissolve yeast in warm water and let
    proof 5 minutes. Put 1 cup (250 ml) flour in a bowl and
    incorporate the yeast mixture. Beat well, cover, and set in
    a warm place for 1 hour. When dough has risen, stir in
    remaining flour, then incorporate the warm milk. Beat well,
    cover, and let rise in a warm place for 45 minutes.

2. To prepare topping, in a skillet, heat olive oil. Add pancetta
    and cook until crisp; drain on paper towels and crumble.
    In fat remaining in skillet, cook onions slowly (about
    30 minutes) until they are very soft but not brown. Add
    sugar and continue cooking until sugars in onions caramel-
    ize. Remove from heat and set aside.

3. Preheat oven to 400°F (205°C). Oil a baking sheet well and
    pour in the dough, which will be rather soupy. Arrange
    onions and pancetta over dough. Dust with Parmesan cheese
    and pepper. Bake until well browned (about 35 minutes).
    Remove from pan; cool at least 10 minutes before cutting
    and serving.

Makes 16 cocktail squares.

GRUYÈRE PUFFS

Imported cheese gives these savory mouthfuls their robust flavor.

¾ cup	milk	175 ml
¾ cup	water	175 ml
½ cup	butter	125 ml
1⅓ cups	unbleached flour	335 ml
¼ tsp	cayenne pepper	¼ tsp
½ tsp	ground white pepper	½ tsp
1 tsp	salt	1 tsp
pinch	nutmeg	pinch
6	eggs	6
1½ cups	grated Gruyère cheese	350 ml
1 tbl	Dijon mustard	1 tbl
1	egg yolk	1
2 tbl	grated Parmesan or Gruyère cheese	2 tbl

1. Preheat oven to 400°F (205°C). Set aside 1 tablespoon of the milk. In a saucepan combine remaining milk with water and butter. Bring to a boil over moderate heat, adjusting heat so that butter is melted by the time the mixture boils. Remove from heat and add flour, cayenne, white pepper, salt, and nutmeg. Stir until smooth, then return to moderate heat and cook 1 minute, stirring constantly.

2. Remove pan from heat and stir in eggs one at a time, beating well after each addition. Stir in Gruyère cheese and mustard. Drop mixture by scant tablespoons onto oiled baking sheet.

3. Whisk together the remaining 1 tablespoon milk and egg yolk. Brush tops of puffs with egg glaze. Dot tops with grated Parmesan cheese. Bake 15 minutes without opening oven door. Check for doneness; puffs should be firm and well browned. Bake a few minutes longer, if necessary. Cool slightly on racks. Serve warm or at room temperature.

Makes 36 puffs.

BASIL-CHEESE SFOGLIA

Cut this cheese pastry into thin strips for easy eating.

1 recipe	Quick Puff Pastry (see page 79)	1 recipe
¾ cup	grated Parmesan cheese	175 ml
½ cup	grated fontina cheese	125 ml
½ cup	grated Jarlsberg cheese	125 ml
1 lb	ricotta cheese	450 g
¾ cup	julienned fresh basil	175 ml
1	egg beaten with 2 tablespoons water, for glaze	1

1. Line a baking sheet with parchment paper. Roll half the puff pastry into a rectangle 6 inches (15 cm) wide by 18 inches (45 cm) long. Place on baking sheet. Stir together cheeses and basil and mound down center of pastry, leaving a 2-inch (5-cm) border on all sides. Brush border with 1 tablespoon water.

2. Roll remaining pastry into same size rectangle and set over first sheet. Press border to seal; with back of knife, create a decorative edge. Brush pastry with egg-water glaze. Chill 1–24 hours, tightly wrapped.

3. An hour before serving, preheat oven to 425°F (220°C). Bake until golden brown (about 35 minutes). Cool 5 minutes before slicing and serving.

Serves 12.

PARTY PLANNING

If you're planning hors d'oeuvres to precede an elaborate dinner, keep them few and simple. Serve a few tempting items that arouse, rather than satiate, the appetite. If the only food you plan to serve at the gathering is hors d'oeuvres, with no dinner afterward, then your guests will need more substantial party fare, particularly if alcohol is served.

QUESADILLAS FRESCAS

A quesadilla is a south-of-the-border grilled cheese sandwich. Prepared with Cheddar, Monterey jack, goat cheese, or Brie layered between two flour tortillas, quesadillas make an appealing hors d'oeuvre served with Salsa Cruda Sabrosa (see page 16).

1 cup	grated Cheddar cheese	250 ml
1 cup	grated Monterey jack cheese	250 ml
12	flour tortillas	12
6	green onions, diced	6
12 sprigs	cilantro (coriander leaves)	12 sprigs
3 tbl	olive oil	3 tbl
as needed	fresh salsa	as needed

1. In a small bowl combine cheeses. Sprinkle a sixth of the cheese mixture on a flour tortilla. Dot with diced green onions and 2 sprigs cilantro. Cover with a second tortilla. Repeat with remaining tortillas.

2. In a 10-inch (25-cm) skillet over medium-high heat, heat 1 teaspoon oil. Cook stuffed tortillas, one by one, adding oil as needed, until very lightly browned and crispy (about 3 minutes). Turn and cook second side until lightly browned and cheese is melted (about 2 minutes).

3. Remove from pan and reserve in a warm oven until all quesadillas are done. Cut each into 6 pieces and serve with salsa.

Serves 12.

QUESADILLA PANTRY

Although quesadillas are traditionally made with only cheese and perhaps chiles, you can add different ingredients to make this Mexican staple more exciting.

The next time you're in the mood for a quesadilla fiesta, experiment with some of these additions from the refrigerator, freezer, or pantry shelf:

In the refrigerator *Flour and corn tortillas, assorted cheeses (Cheddar, Monterey jack, asadero, goat cheese, Brie), green onions, tomatoes, mushrooms, bell peppers, jicama, zucchini, ripe avocados, fresh cilantro, fresh salsa, sour cream*

In the freezer *Cooked, shredded, seasoned chicken, beef, or pork*

On the shelf *Canned green chiles, canned black olives, canned tomatillos, bottled chile sauce*

BAGUETTE MELTS

Serve these no-fuss cheese snacks hot from the oven. For variety, use Swiss or jack cheese and top with bits of smoked turkey or ham.

½ lb	grated Cheddar cheese	225 g
1 can (4½ oz)	chopped ripe olives	1 can (130 g)
1 can (2 oz)	diced pimientos	1 can (60 g)
4	green onions, finely chopped	4
½ cup	mayonnaise	125 ml
1½ tbl	prepared horseradish	1½ tbl
1	large baguette, sliced diagonally	1

1. Blend cheese, olives, pimientos, green onions, mayonnaise, and horseradish.

2. Spoon about 1 tablespoon cheese mixture onto each baguette slice.

3. Broil until cheese starts to melt. Serve hot.

Makes about 36 slices.

APPETIZERS FROM THE MICROWAVE

With a microwave oven and a few simple ingredients you probably already have on hand, you can make a platter of appetizers in minutes. Once you try these, you're bound to come up with some interesting combinations of your own. The following combinations are given without specific amounts of ingredients, so prepare them to suit your own taste.

- *Top rich, buttery crackers with shredded Muenster or Monterey jack cheese. Microwave on full power until cheese has melted (about 15 seconds), then garnish with finely chopped chives.*

- *Top water crackers with almond butter and thinly sliced sweet onion or red onion. Microwave on full power until warm (about 15 seconds), then garnish with toasted slivered almonds.*

- *Top melba toast with tuna salad and slices of Swiss cheese. Microwave on full power until cheese is melted (about 15 seconds), then garnish with snippets of fresh dill.*

- *In a microwave-safe bowl combine equal parts of grated sharp Cheddar cheese and canned clams. Microwave on full power until cheese is melted (about 1 minute). Blend with a spoon, season to taste with hot-pepper sauce, and serve with an assortment of crackers and deli breads.*

- *In a microwave-safe bowl combine pineapple preserves and prepared mustard to taste. Spoon over sliced turkey sausage links and microwave on full power until sausages sizzle (about 1 minute). Stir to coat sausages with mustard mixture and serve with small skewers.*

FONTINA FRITTERS

Crisp on the outside, with a molten cheese center, these fritters are a heavenly mouthful. The batter can be made ahead, but the cheese must be fried at the last minute.

¾ lb	chilled fontina cheese, not too ripe	350 g
¼ cup	dry white wine	60 ml
2	eggs, separated	2
1 tsp	minced garlic	1 tsp
1 tsp	baking powder	1 tsp
1½ cups	unbleached flour	350 ml
as needed	salt	as needed
2½ tbl	olive oil	2½ tbl
½–⅔ cup	ice water	125–150 ml
as needed	peanut oil, for deep-frying	as needed
½ cup	minced fresh basil	125 ml

1. Cut cheese into 1-inch (2.5 cm) cubes. In a bowl whisk together wine, egg yolks, and garlic. Whisk in baking powder, flour, and 1 teaspoon of the salt. Whisk in oil, then add enough of the ice water to make a thick but pourable batter, about the consistency of pancake batter. Let rest at room temperature for 2 hours.

2. When ready to serve, heat 2 inches (5 cm) of oil in a frying pan to 360°F (180°C). Beat egg whites with a pinch of salt until stiff but not dry. Fold into batter along with minced basil.

3. Dip cheese chunks into batter. Allow excess batter to drip off; fry chunks in oil until uniformly golden. Drain fritters on paper towels and salt lightly. Serve fritters immediately.

Makes about 16 fritters.

SESAME WINGS

Although chicken drummettes resemble miniature chicken legs, these tasty appetizers are actually the second joint of the chicken wing (with the wing tip removed). Toast the sesame seeds in a heavy-bottomed skillet over high heat, shaking the pan until the seeds are golden brown and a fragrantly nutty aroma fills the air (about 5 minutes).

½ cup	olive oil	125 ml
½ cup	sherry	125 ml
4 tbl	soy sauce	4 tbl
4 tbl	lemon juice	4 tbl
2 cloves	garlic, minced	2 cloves
4 tbl	toasted sesame seed	4 tbl
2 lb	chicken drummettes	900 g
as needed	salt	as needed

1. In a blender combine oil, sherry, soy sauce, lemon juice, garlic, and sesame seed. Process until smooth.

2. Wash drummettes and pat dry. Salt lightly. Place in a large bowl and cover with sherry marinade. Refrigerate for at least 1 hour.

3. Preheat broiler. Broil drummettes 5 inches (12.5 cm) from heat for 7 minutes per side, basting once on each side with marinade.

Makes about 20 drummettes.

CAJUN POPCORN

The popcornlike texture of this fried shrimp appetizer is delightfully addictive. If you can't find corn flour at a natural food store or specialty market, substitute equal parts of fine cornmeal and unbleached flour.

Seasoned Corn Flour Coating

3 cups	corn flour	700 ml
2 tsp	salt	2 tsp
¼ tsp	ground white pepper	¼ tsp
½ tsp	cayenne pepper	½ tsp
as needed	peanut oil, for deep-frying	as needed
1 lb	small or medium shrimp, peeled and deveined	450 g
1 tsp each	salt and cayenne pepper	1 tsp each
⅛ tsp	ground white pepper	⅛ tsp
½ tsp	garlic powder	½ tsp
4 tbl	water	4 tbl

1. To prepare flour coating, in a large bowl thoroughly blend all ingredients. Set aside.

2. Preheat wok over medium-high heat until hot. Pour in oil to a depth of 2 inches (5 cm) and heat to 375°F (190°C).

3. In a bowl combine shrimp, salt, cayenne, white pepper, and garlic powder. Add 2 tablespoons of the water and blend. Divide mixture between 2 bowls.

4. Add 2 tablespoons of flour coating to 1 bowl of the shrimp mixture; blend well. Pour entire mixture into large bowl of corn flour coating and toss gently. With a skimmer scoop out shrimp, shaking excess coating into bowl. Add shrimp to hot oil in batches, and deep-fry until brown (about 2–4 minutes, depending on size of shrimp). Remove and keep warm. Repeat with remaining shrimp mixture. Serve hot.

Serves 8.

Effortless Hors d'Oeuvres

How can such elegant food be so easy to prepare? With a little planning, you can have an eye-catching array of appetizers and hors d'oeuvres in just minutes.

Crostini of Salami and Parmesan Cheese Cut a baguette into ¼ inch (.6 cm) slices. Top with a slice of salami and grated Parmesan cheese. Bake in a preheated 350°F (175°C) oven until warm (2–3 minutes).

Grilled Sausage with Spicy Mustard Grill or broil links of mild Italian sausage; cut into pieces and serve on skewers, accompanied with your favorite spicy mustard.

Endive Spears with Guacamole, Bay Shrimp, and Salsa Trim root end from a head of Belgian endive; separate endive into spears. Place ½ teaspoon prepared guacamole near cut end and add 2 or 3 bay shrimp and ¼ teaspoon bottled salsa.

Smoked Salmon Mousse In a food processor, purée 4 ounces (115 g) smoked salmon, 4 ounces (115 g) softened cream cheese, and juice of ½ lemon. Place in a small dish and serve with baguette slices or crackers.

Steamed Potatoes with Aioli Steam 2 pounds (900 g) tiny red potatoes until tender when pierced with a knife (30 to 35 minutes). Cool slightly. While potatoes are steaming, prepare aioli by mincing 3 cloves garlic and stirring it into 1 cup (250 ml) homemade or bottled mayonnaise. Spoon aioli into a bowl. Slice potatoes into halves and arrange around bowl of aioli.

Cucumber Rounds with Sour Cream and Chutney Slice English cucumbers crosswise about ¼ inch (.6 cm) thick. Top each slice with 1 teaspoon sour cream and ½ teaspoon prepared chutney.

GOLDEN SHRIMP PÂTÉ ROUNDS

A spicy shrimp mixture atop crusty French bread slices turns golden when fried. The Thai fish sauce is available in most Asian markets.

½ lb	raw shrimp, peeled and deveined	225 g
1 tbl	butter	1 tbl
1	green onion, chopped	1
1 tsp	Thai fish sauce	1 tsp
¼ tsp	salt	¼ tsp
pinch	ground white pepper	pinch
1	baguette, sliced ½ inch (1.25 cm) thick	1
as needed	peanut oil, for deep-frying	as needed
as needed	butter lettuce and mint leaves	as needed

1. In a food processor or blender, combine shrimp, butter, and green onion and process to a smooth, fluffy paste. Add fish sauce, salt, and pepper and blend thoroughly. Set aside.

2. Toast bread slices in a low oven until crisp (about 10 minutes).

3. Spread shrimp mixture about ¼-inch (.6-cm) thick on each bread slice.

4. Fill a wok with oil to a depth of 1 inch (2.5 cm). Heat oil to 350°F (175°C), then reduce heat to low. Add a few toasts, shrimp side down, and fry until golden brown (about 1 minute). Turn and cook 45 seconds–1 minute on other side. Remove, drain on paper towels and repeat with remaining toasts. Garnish with lettuce leaves and mint leaves.

Makes 18 toasts.

PORK SATÉ

These skewers of thinly sliced pork are easy to prepare and grill very quickly. Strips of chicken breast may be substituted for the pork.

⅓ cup	medium or thick coconut milk	85 ml
¼ tsp	turmeric	¼ tsp
1 tsp	roughly chopped lemongrass stalks	1 tsp
1 tsp	Thai fish sauce	1 tsp
½ lb	boneless pork loin or leg	225 g

1. In a small skillet or saucepan, combine coconut milk, turmeric, lemongrass, and fish sauce. Bring to a boil, turn off heat, and allow to cool.

2. Slice pork ⅛ inch (.3 cm) thick across the grain and cut into 1-inch (2.5-cm) squares. Marinate pork in coconut mixture 30 minutes. Thread meat on skewers, allowing 2 or 3 pork slices per skewer and stretching meat out in an even thin layer. Grill over a hot fire until lightly browned on both sides (about 2 minutes per side).

Serves 4.

EAST-WEST WONTONS

Fried, these pork-filled appetizers go well with tangy sweet-and-sour sauces or mustard dips; steamed, they are best with soy sauce dips. You can substitute beef, lamb, or dark meat from chicken or turkey for the pork.

1 lb	wonton skins	450 g
1 lb	seasoned ground pork	450 g
as needed	peanut oil, for deep-frying (optional)	as needed

1. Have at hand a small bowl of water with a brush for sealing edges. Peel off 2 or 3 wonton skins and place on the work surface, with one corner (the "south") pointing toward you. Keep remaining skins covered with a towel to prevent drying.

2. Place a scant teaspoon of ground pork just south of center of skin. Brush near edges lightly with water and fold south corner over filling to within ½ inch (1.25 cm) of north corner. Press edges to seal. Pick up east and west corners and bring together at south end. Pinch or twist slightly to seal corners together. Repeat with remaining skins and filling.

3. Keep finished wontons covered with a towel to prevent them from drying, or freeze on a baking sheet and transfer to plastic bags when fully frozen. Boil in plain or lightly salted water before adding to hot soup, steam 6–8 minutes to make a simple appetizer, or deep-fry in 375°F (190°C) oil until golden brown and crisp (about 3–4 minutes).

Makes 60 wontons.

PEANUT-CHICKEN SKEWERS

Strips of chicken flavored with a sweet and peppery peanut sauce are threaded on skewers with red peppers and grilled until crisp and juicy. Note that the chicken must marinate in the sauce overnight.

6	chicken breast halves, boned and skinned	6
1 cup	crunchy peanut butter	250 ml
1/3 cup	chopped cilantro (coriander leaves)	85 ml
1/2 cup	prepared chili sauce	125 ml
1 tbl	salt	1 tbl
1/2 tsp	cayenne pepper	1/2 tsp
1/2 tsp	freshly ground black pepper	1/2 tsp
1/4 cup	lemon juice	60 ml
1/4 cup	firmly packed brown sugar	60 ml
1/2 cup	soy sauce	125 ml
8	green onions	8
3 tbl	minced garlic	3 tbl
24	6- to 8-inch (15- to 20-cm) bamboo skewers	24
2	bell peppers, red or green, cut into 1/2-inch (1.25-cm) cubes	2
as needed	minced parsley, for garnish	as needed

1. Slice each breast half lengthwise into 4 strips; set aside.

2. In a stainless steel, glass, or ceramic bowl, combine peanut butter, cilantro, chili sauce, salt, cayenne, black pepper, lemon juice, brown sugar, soy sauce, green onions, and garlic. Add chicken strips, cover, and let marinate in refrigerator overnight or up to 2 days.

3. Soak bamboo skewers in water for 30 minutes and drain. Preheat broiler or prepare a charcoal fire. Thread chicken strips onto skewers, alternating with pepper cubes. Broil or grill for 5–6 minutes, turning once. Serve garnished with minced parsley.

Makes 24 skewers.

MEATBALLS WRAPPED IN CRISPY NOODLES

This appetizer presents tender pork in a crunchy wrapper, with a nugget of preserved egg in the center.

1 lb	ground or minced pork	450 g
1 tbl each	minced coriander root and garlic	1 tbl each
1 tsp each	salt and freshly ground black pepper	1 tsp each
1	egg	1
1 tbl	unbleached flour	1 tbl
1 cup	finely chopped water chestnuts, bamboo shoots, or black mushrooms	250 ml
1	yolk of hard-cooked egg	1
½ lb	dried thin egg noodles	225 g
as needed	peanut oil, for deep-frying	as needed
as needed	soy sauce	as needed
as needed	chile sauce	as needed

1. Combine pork, coriander root, garlic, salt, pepper, egg, flour, and chopped vegetables and blend thoroughly. If using a food processor, chop vegetables and seasonings together first, then add pork and egg and grind to a smooth paste.

2. Form meat mixture into 1-inch (2.5-cm) balls, embedding a small piece of cooked egg yolk in the center of each.

3. Soak noodles in warm water just long enough to soften; drain. Wrap each meatball in a few strands of noodle, enclosing ball completely.

4. Bring oil in frying pan to 360°F (180°C) and fry balls a few at a time until golden brown. Cut one open after frying to be sure meat is thoroughly cooked; if not, reduce oil temperature and increase cooking time. Serve with soy sauce and chile sauce for dipping.

Makes 36 meatballs.

Stuffed Broiled Mushrooms

If you use medium-sized mushrooms, serve these succulent mouthfuls as finger food; if you use large mushrooms, your guests will appreciate plates and forks. Mushrooms with stems that are slightly pulled away from the undersides of the caps are easiest to stem and stuff. This appetizer can be frozen before final broiling, if desired.

12–16	mushrooms	12–16
1 tsp	olive oil	1 tsp
1	onion, finely chopped	1
1 cup	bread crumbs, finely ground	1 cup
¼ cup	minced almonds	60 ml
1 tbl	sherry	1 tbl
¼ tsp	marjoram	¼ tsp
to taste	freshly ground black pepper	to taste

1. Preheat broiler. Remove stems from mushrooms by wiggling at base (stems should pop out). Chop stems finely and set aside.

2. Place caps with open side down on baking sheet and broil for 2 minutes or until caps become wrinkled and begin to weep moisture. Let cool. Keep broiler hot.

3. Heat oil in skillet and sauté onion until soft, then add the chopped mushroom stems. Cook until mushrooms begin to weep moisture (about 8 minutes). Add bread crumbs, almonds, sherry, marjoram, and pepper; cook 1 minute longer.

4. Stuff bread crumb filling into mushroom caps and place filled side up on baking sheet. Broil until light brown. Serve hot.

Makes 12 large- or 16 medium-sized stuffed mushrooms.

CRISP-BAKED POTATO SHELLS

Serve these crispy shells au naturel or dressed up with one of the toppings suggested below.

6 medium	baking potatoes	6 medium
1/4 cup	butter	60 ml
1/4 tsp	paprika	1/4 tsp
pinch	ground white pepper	pinch

1. Preheat oven to 400°F (205°C). Scrub potatoes, pat dry, and rub skins lightly with a little of the butter. Pierce potatoes in several places with a fork.

2. Bake potatoes until tender when pierced (45 minutes–1 hour). When cool enough to handle, cut in halves lengthwise and scoop out potato, leaving a thin shell about 1/8 inch (.3 cm) thick. Reserve potato for other dishes.

3. Place shells on a baking sheet. Melt butter in a small pan with paprika and white pepper. Stir. Brush insides of potato shells with butter mixture. Bake potato shells until crispy (about 15–18 minutes).

Makes 12 shells.

TOPPINGS FOR BAKED POTATO SHELLS

Potato skins like the ones in the preceding recipe are one of the most popular, economical, versatile appetizers you can prepare. Before the second baking, sprinkle the shells with grated Cheddar cheese, crumbled bacon, or chopped green onions or chives. For a Southwestern flavor, sprinkle with grated jack cheese, sliced jalapeño chiles, and chopped black olives. After the shells have baked, garnish with sour cream, yogurt, Salsa Cruda Sabrosa, or Fiesta Guacamole (see page 16).

PLATE FOOD

Fancy offerings like the ones in this section deserve plates and forks. From miniature tarts rich with Cheddar and cream (see page 73) to lusciously tender oysters baked on a bed of rock salt (see page 90), these are the kinds of hors d'oeuvres that make a host's reputation.

Savory Cheddar Tartlets

Eggs, cream, and sharp Cheddar cheese bake to golden perfection in these tiny cocktail tarts. Use fresh or frozen packaged pastry shells or, if you prefer, prepare the shells from your own favorite pastry dough.

2 (10-inch)	prepared pastry shells, unbaked	2 (25-cm)
4	eggs, lightly beaten	4
2 cups	whipping cream	500 ml
to taste	salt, freshly ground black pepper, nutmeg, and cayenne pepper	to taste
½ lb	sharp Cheddar cheese, cubed	225 g
¼ cup	chopped chives	60 ml

1. Preheat oven to 350°F (175°C). Use pastry shells to line 24 2-inch (5-cm) tartlet pans. Chill 30 minutes.

2. To prepare filling, in a small bowl blend eggs and whipping cream. Add salt, black pepper, nutmeg, and cayenne to taste. Stir well.

3. Divide cheese cubes among tartlet shells and top with cream mixture. Bake tartlets until well browned (12–15 minutes). Cool slightly, then garnish with chopped chives and serve.

Makes 24 tartlets.

ZUCCHINI GRATIN

For this quick, delicious recipe you will need about 1½ pounds (680 grams) of zucchini.

4 cups	zucchini, finely grated	900 ml
½ cup	unbleached flour	125 ml
¼ cup each	grated mozzarella, fontina, Gruyère, and Parmesan cheese	60 ml each
2 tbl	chopped fresh basil	2 tbl
4	eggs, lightly beaten	4
to taste	salt and freshly ground black pepper	to taste
as needed	olive oil	as needed

1. Preheat oven to 375°F (190°C). In a large bowl combine zucchini, flour, cheeses, basil, eggs, and salt and pepper.

2. Press mixture into a buttered 11- by 15-inch (27.5- by 37.5-cm) baking dish. Bake until firm and browned (25–30 minutes).

3. Remove from oven and preheat broiler. Drizzle top of mixture with olive oil and broil just until the top browns. Cool slightly, then cut into 36 squares and serve.

Makes 36 squares.

PARTY BUFFETS WITH EYE APPEAL

Here are some tips for a party buffet that looks as good as it tastes:
- *Choose foods that will hold up well over time on a platter or in a chafing dish.*
- *Select dishes with a pleasing variety of colors, flavors, and textures, avoiding combinations that clash.*
- *Keep backup food ready in the kitchen for replacing dishes on the buffet table that become depleted or untidy-looking. Do any sprucing up of serving dishes in the kitchen, not at the buffet table.*

ANGOURASALATA

White wine vinegar adds a distinctive note to this traditional Greek salad of cucumbers in yogurt (see photo on page 10).

2	English cucumbers, halved, seeded, and cut into ½-inch (1.25-cm) dice	2
1 tbl	salt	1 tbl
2 tbl	white wine vinegar	2 tbl
2 cups	plain yogurt	500 ml
½ tsp	sugar	½ tsp
3 tbl	minced red onion	3 tbl
1	green onion, minced	1
2 tsp	minced garlic	2 tsp
2 tbl	minced fresh dill	2 tbl
2 tbl	olive oil	2 tbl
to taste	salt	to taste
as needed	freshly ground black pepper	as needed
as needed	fresh dill sprigs, for garnish	as needed

1. Place diced cucumbers in a large colander; sprinkle with salt and 1 tablespoon of the vinegar. Toss to blend. Let drain 30 minutes, then rinse and pat dry.

2. Transfer cucumbers to a large bowl. Add remaining tablespoon vinegar, yogurt, sugar, red onion, green onion, garlic, dill, and oil. Toss to blend, then season with salt. Cover and refrigerate 30 minutes. To serve, garnish with black pepper and dill sprigs.

Serves 8.

RATATOUILLE PUFFS

Airy puff pastry is the base for this appetizer.

1	eggplant, diced	1
1 tbl	salt	1 tbl
8 tbl	olive oil	8 tbl
1	onion, diced	1
2 cloves	garlic, minced	2 cloves
2	zucchini, diced	2
1	yellow bell pepper, diced	1
8	tomatoes, peeled, seeded, and quartered	8
1 tbl	dried basil	1 tbl
1 tsp each	dried oregano and thyme	1 tsp each
1 recipe	Quick Puff Pastry (see page 79)	1 recipe
1	egg, beaten	1

1. Place eggplant in a colander and sprinkle with 2 teaspoons of the salt. Let sit 30 minutes. Rinse and pat dry. In a skillet over medium heat, add 6 tablespoons of the oil; cook the eggplant in batches until lightly browned (about 5 minutes). Remove to a platter and reserve.

2. Preheat oven to 425°F (220°C). Add remaining oil to skillet; cook onion and garlic until translucent (about 5 minutes). Return eggplant to skillet. Stir in zucchini, bell pepper, tomatoes, basil, oregano, thyme, and remaining salt. Simmer, stirring occasionally, (about 20 minutes); keep warm.

3. Line a baking sheet with parchment paper. Cut Quick Puff Pastry into twelve 4- by 3-inch (10- by 7.5-cm) rectangles. Place rectangles on baking sheet. Brush tops of rectangles with beaten egg. Bake until brown and crisp (about 24 minutes). Remove from oven and halve each rectangle horizontally. Place about ½ cup (125 ml) ratatouille on bottom half of each rectangle, top with remaining rectangle, and serve immediately.

Serves 12.

SMORREBROD: DANISH SANDWICHES

Literally "buttered bread," the word smorrebrod actually refers to an endless collection of both simple and elaborate open-faced sandwiches you eat with a fork (see photo on page 4). The Danes eat them for lunch, but half-portions make splendidly hearty hors d'oeuvres.

Use a sharp knife to cut thin slices of Danish-style pumpernickel (preferably day-old) for the base of the sandwiches. To keep the bread from getting soggy, spread the slices lightly with softened butter (salted or unsalted, depending upon the other ingredients) or butter flavored with herbs. Garnish with a light touch and an artful eye, making the sandwiches as colorful and appealing as possible. Eight or ten different choices is not too many for a typical smorrebrod. Arrange the sandwiches on a large tray or on wooden cutting boards. Start with these popular combinations and then use your imagination to create some new favorites of your own:

- *Salted butter, paper-thin slices of sweet red onion, capers*

- *Horseradish butter, thinly sliced cucumber, sliced hard-boiled egg*

- *Unsalted butter, sliced Havarti cheese, sliced radish, whole caraway seeds*

- *Dill butter, baby shrimp, lemon slices, fresh dill leaves*

- *Unsalted butter, creamed pickled herring, sliced onion*

QUICK PUFF PASTRY

Making classic French puff pastry is never "quick" but, using this method, you can get very similar results with half the time and effort. Use this version to make Parmesan Twists (see page 31), Basil-Cheese Sfoglia (see page 51), and Ratatouille Puffs (see page 76).

1⅓ cups	unbleached flour	335 ml
⅔ cup	cake or pastry flour	150 ml
1 tsp	salt	1 tsp
14 tbl	unsalted butter, cut in pieces and frozen for 30 minutes	14 tbl
½–¾ cup	very cold whipping cream	125–175 ml

1. Combine flours and salt in a bowl or on a marble work surface. Cut in butter coarsely until it is reduced to ¼-inch (.6-cm) bits. Add ½ cup (125 ml) cream and mix gently using hands, adding additional cream if necessary, until mixture just forms a ball. Amount of cream will vary depending on humidity and type of flour.

2. Roll dough out on a lightly floured surface into a rectangle 8 by 20 inches (20 by 50 cm). Fold the two 8-inch (20-cm) ends toward the center until they meet in the middle. Then fold one half over the other. Wrap in plastic and refrigerate dough 1 hour. Repeat the rolling and folding process twice, refrigerating the dough 1 hour after each time. Repeat rolling and folding one more time, then roll out and cut as desired.

Makes about 1 pound (450 g) puff pastry.

ANTIPASTO MISTO

Italian antipasto, so named because it was traditionally served before the meal (pasto), can be expanded for large parties or last-minute guests by increasing the amount of the components. The pasta salad is an Italian-American innovation.

Pasta Salad

2	tomatoes, diced	2
½ lb	mozzarella cheese, cubed	225 g
1	red onion, minced	1
2 cloves	garlic, minced	2 cloves
1 bunch	basil, chopped	1 bunch
3½ tbl	red wine vinegar	3½ tbl
2 tbl	olive oil	2 tbl
1 tsp	salt	1 tsp
1 tsp	freshly ground black pepper	1 tsp
4 cups	cooked, drained pasta shells	900 ml
½ lb	salami, thinly sliced	225 g
½ lb	mortadella, thinly sliced	225 g
¼ lb	Provolone cheese, sliced	115 g
12 oz	Niçoise olives	350 g
1 jar (8 oz)	peperoncini	1 jar (225 g)
1 jar (6 oz)	artichoke hearts, drained	1 jar (170 g)
1 each	red and green bell pepper, cut in strips	1 each
as needed	marinated onions	as needed

1. To prepare Pasta Salad, in a 3-quart (2.7-l) bowl stir together tomatoes, mozzarella cheese, red onion, garlic, basil, vinegar, oil, salt, and pepper. Add pasta and toss well.

2. To arrange for serving, mound pasta salad in center of platter and arrange remaining ingredients around it.

Serves 8.

LAMB CAKES

These ground lamb patties are irresistible served with a colorful hot garnish of pimientos and parsley.

1	egg	1
¼ cup	soft bread crumbs	60 ml
½ tsp	garlic salt	½ tsp
⅛ tsp	cinnamon	⅛ tsp
1 jar (4 oz)	pimientos, drained and finely chopped	1 jar (115 g)
1 lb	ground lamb	450 g
1 tbl each	butter and olive oil	1 tbl each
1 tsp	lemon juice	1 tsp
1 tbl	water	1 tbl
¼ cup	chopped parsley	60 ml

1. In a medium bowl beat egg slightly, then mix in crumbs, garlic salt, cinnamon, and ¼ cup (60 ml) of the chopped pimientos. Lightly mix in lamb; shape mixture into 8 patties.

2. In a large frying pan over medium heat, melt butter with oil; brown lamb patties slowly, turning once and cooking about 6 minutes on each side. Remove patties to a warm serving dish and keep them warm.

3. Pour off and discard all but about 1 tablespoon of the pan drippings. Add remaining pimientos, lemon juice, water, and parsley. Cook, stirring to incorporate brown bits from pan, just until mixture is heated through. Spoon over lamb patties and serve.

Serves 8.

PANTRY PIZZAS

Many of the ingredients needed for this quick, easy appetizer are already in your pantry, refrigerator, and freezer. The toppings can be as varied as your imagination—salami or pepperoni slices, bits of turkey ham, canned clams, pineapple chunks, wedges of marinated artichoke hearts. Keep your eyes open for possibilities the next time you're shopping. Use this basic recipe to make pizza for one or a hundred.

For each pizza:

one (8-inch)	pita bread	one (20-cm)
1 tsp	olive oil	1 tsp
¼ cup	seeded and chopped tomatoes	60 ml
	or	
1–2 tbl	tomato paste	1–2 tbl
¼ tsp	finely chopped garlic	¼ tsp
to taste	fresh or dried herbs (oregano, thyme, basil, and rosemary, singly or in combination)	to taste
3–4 tbl	freshly grated Parmesan cheese	3–4 tbl

1. Preheat oven to 450°F (230°C). Place the pita bread on a baking sheet and brush lightly with oil.

2. Top with tomatoes or spread with tomato paste.

3. Scatter garlic and your choice of fresh or dried herbs over top. Sprinkle with Parmesan cheese.

4. Bake until crust is crisp and lightly browned (about 10–15 minutes).

Makes 1 pizza.

GOOD FORTUNE CHICKEN

Bite-sized pieces of chicken fried inside a wrapper of paper or foil are a popular Chinese appetizer. Marinades for the chicken can be elaborate mixtures of condiments or a simple combination like this one.

1	chicken breast half, skinned, boned, and cut into ½-inch (1.25-cm) cubes	1
1 tbl each	soy sauce and Shaoxing wine or dry sherry	1 tbl each
1 tbl	grated ginger	1 tbl
1 tsp	Asian sesame oil	1 tsp
as needed	peanut oil, for deep-frying	as needed

1. Combine chicken, soy sauce, wine, ginger, and sesame oil; marinate for 30 minutes at room temperature or up to several hours in the refrigerator. Cut eighteen 4-inch (10-cm) squares of parchment paper or aluminum foil.

2. Place a square of paper on work surface, with one corner pointing toward you ("south"). Place 2 or 3 chicken cubes across center of square. Fold south corner over chicken to ½ inch (1.25 cm) from north corner. Crease fold. Fold in east and west corners so that they overlap each other, and crease edges. Fold whole package toward north, forming an envelope. Tuck north corner into envelope and crease to seal. Repeat with remaining packages.

3. In a wok or other deep pan, heat peanut oil to 375°F (190°C). Fry chicken packages, a few at a time, for about 1 minute (parchment paper will turn golden brown). To make unwrapping easier, slit open each package along folded edge before serving.

Makes 18 packages.

CANTONESE PORK DUMPLINGS

These tiny treasures make savory hors d'oeuvres (see photo on page 11). Siu mai wrappers (very thin noodlelike dough rounds) are available in most Asian markets.

½ cup	shredded cabbage (green variety)	125 ml
½ tsp	salt	½ tsp
1 lb	boneless pork	450 g
¼ cup each	minced green onion and bamboo shoots	60 ml each
1 tbl	minced fresh ginger	1 tbl
as needed	soy sauce and dry sherry	as needed
1 tsp	sesame oil	1 tsp
1	egg	1
1 tsp	cornstarch	1 tsp
24	siu mai wrappers, packaged or homemade	24

1. To prepare stuffing toss cabbage with salt and place in a colander to drain 30 minutes. Squeeze out excess moisture. Mince pork to a fine texture. In a bowl, combine pork, cabbage, green onions, bamboo shoots, ginger, 2 table-spoons each soy sauce and dry sherry, sesame oil, egg, and cornstarch.

2. Place a wrapper in the palm of one hand and spoon 1 tablespoon of stuffing into the center. Gently fold up sides of wrapper around stuffing, pressing wrapper against stuffing in 4 or 5 places. Pick up remaining folds of wrapper and press them in against stuffing, shaping dumpling into an open-topped cylinder. Try to avoid large pleats, which will be tougher after steaming than tiny folds.

3. Steam on a bamboo steamer with a lattice cover 20–25 minutes. Before serving, drizzle with a little soy sauce mixed with sesame oil.

Makes 24 dumplings.

Prawns with Islander Plum Sauce

The perfect partner for prawns is this tangy sweet-and-sour plum sauce.

Islander Plum Sauce

2 lb	purple plums	900 g
¼ cup	fresh lemon juice	60 ml
½ cup	red wine vinegar	125 ml
¼ cup	Japanese plum wine or sake	60 ml
1 tbl	Dijon mustard	1 tbl
to taste	cayenne pepper	to taste
to taste	salt	to taste
3 lb	prawns, boiled and shelled	1.4 kg
2 tbl	minced parsley	2 tbl
1 tsp	grated lemon zest	1 tsp

1. To prepare Islander Plum Sauce, cut a cross in the bottom of each plum. Plunge into boiling water briefly, then into a bowl of ice water. Peel the plums (skins should peel off easily) and pit them. In a food processor or blender, combine plums and lemon juice and process until smooth. Stir in vinegar, plum wine, and mustard. Season with cayenne and salt. Set aside.

2. Arrange prawns on a serving platter. Combine parsley and lemon zest and sprinkle over prawns. Serve with Islander Plum Sauce and cocktail picks.

Serves 10.

Making a Case for Vegetables

You can transform many vegetables into attractive, tasty appetizers. Hollow out small pumpkins, eggplants, bell peppers, or large tomatoes or onions to hold dips, sauces, or crudités. Fill snow peas, endive spears, or hollowed-out cherry tomatoes with a creamy cheese or seafood mixture.

OYSTERS ROCKEFELLER-STYLE

Herbs enliven this variation on an east-coast classic.

24	large oysters in their shells	24
1 cup	spinach leaves, coarsely chopped	250 ml
6 leaves	romaine lettuce, coarsely chopped	6 leaves
1 bunch	watercress, coarsely chopped	1 bunch
¼ cup	parsley, coarsely chopped	60 ml
¼ cup	coarsely chopped green onion tops	60 ml
1 stalk	celery, coarsely chopped	1 stalk
¾ cup	unsalted butter, softened	175 ml
1 clove	garlic, minced	1 clove
½ cup	dry bread crumbs	125 ml
½ tsp each	basil and ground fennel seed	½ tsp each
1 tsp	hot-pepper sauce	1 tsp
¼ cup	anise-flavored liqueur	60 ml
to taste	salt and freshly ground black pepper	to taste
1 lb	rock salt	450 g

1. Shuck oysters and wash sand and grit from larger bottom shells.

2. In a food processor or blender, finely chop spinach, lettuce, watercress, parsley, green onions, and celery; place in a mixing bowl. Put the butter in processor bowl; cream with garlic, bread crumbs, basil, fennel seed, and hot-pepper sauce. Add finely chopped greens and liqueur. Process until no lumps of butter remain. Taste and add salt and pepper if needed.

3. Place oven rack at top of oven; preheat oven to 500°F (260°C). Place oyster shells on a ½-inch (1.25- cm) layer of rock salt in an ovenproof pan. Drop an oyster into each shell and cover with 1 tablespoon of butter mixture. Bake until sauce bubbles and oysters plump (about 10 minutes). Preheat broiler; broil oysters just until lightly browned (about 30 seconds).

Serves 4.

MINTED SCALLOPS

Most party-supply and gourmet food stores carry an assortment of festive skewers and toothpicks to accompany cocktail fare. Serve the scallops in a serving bowl with skewers or toothpicks alongside, or present the scallops as a seafood cocktail, complete with shrimp forks. If you prefer, save and clean the extra clamshells from Italian Baked Clams (see page 94) and spoon the scallop mixture into the shells for a distinctive shellfish cocktail (see photo on page 93).

1½ lb	fresh bay or sea scallops	680 g
½ cup	loosely packed mint leaves, minced	125 ml
2 tbl	minced Italian parsley	2 tbl
2 cups	extra virgin olive oil	500 ml
as needed	lemon juice	as needed
1 tsp	grated lemon zest	1 tsp
1 cup	seeded and diced tomato	250 ml
2 tbl	minced shallot	2 tbl
as needed	salt	as needed
as needed	freshly ground black pepper	as needed

1. If using bay scallops, leave whole. If using sea scallops, trim away tough muscle and cut scallops into ½-inch (1.25-cm) dice. Transfer to a stainless steel, glass, or enamel bowl; add mint, parsley, oil, 3 tablespoons lemon juice, zest, tomato, shallot, 1 teaspoon salt, and ¼ teaspoon pepper.

2. Cover and refrigerate at least 45 minutes or up to 1 day; remove from refrigerator 30 minutes before serving. Taste and add salt, pepper, and lemon juice if needed. Transfer to a serving bowl or to individual clamshells.

Serves 16.

ITALIAN BAKED CLAMS

Roasted red bell peppers add color and zest to this dish (see photo on page 93).

64	fresh clams, scrubbed thoroughly	64
2 tbl	cornmeal	2 tbl
2	roasted red bell peppers	2
2 cups	dry white wine	500 ml
½ cup	chopped onion	125 ml
3 tbl	minced parsley	3 tbl
2 tbl	minced basil	2 tbl
1 tbl	minced garlic	1 tbl
as needed	olive oil	as needed
1 cup	seasoned bread crumbs	250 ml

1. In a pot, place clams and cornmeal; add water to cover. Refrigerate 4 hours.

2. Preheat oven to 400°F (205°C). Cut peppers into thin strips. Drain clams and place in roasting pan with wine and onion. Cover and bake 10 minutes. Uncover and transfer opened clams to a bowl. Cover roasting pan and return to oven for 3–4 minutes. Uncover and transfer remaining opened clams to bowl. Discard any unopened clams.

3. Remove clams from shell and return to bowl along with their juices. Separate shells at the hinge and discard half the shells, or save them for another use.

4. Add parsley, basil, garlic, and ¾ cup (175 ml) oil to clams; stir to blend. Cover and refrigerate.

5. Preheat broiler. Place a clam in each half shell and top each clam with a sliver of red pepper. Dust with seasoned bread crumbs and drizzle lightly with oil. Broil until lightly browned (about 3 minutes). Serve immediately.

Makes 64 clams.

INDEX

Note: Page numbers in italics refer to photos.